THE NATURALISTIC OF THINGS ARE THE LEAVES OF HEAVEN

It does not matter what god you praise, what matters is, are you "happy" with your "life"

Ameal Jones III

authorHOUSE®

AuthorHouse™
1663 Liberty Drive
Bloomington, IN 47403
www.authorhouse.com
Phone: 1-800-839-8640

First published by AuthorHouse 1/25/2010

ISBN: 978-1-4490-6288-0 (e)
ISBN: 978-1-4490-6287-3 (sc)

Printed in the United States of America
Bloomington, Indiana

This book is printed on acid-free paper.

Eudaimonism—A system of ethics that evaluates actions in terms of their capacity to produce "happiness." We need to fix our own problems and stop worrying about "God." Can we have a beautiful religion without using or blaming God or the gods for our selfish, humanistic problems? The mind is God, once you lose your mind you lose (power source) the God.

The mind is the greatest force on earth. He who has controlled his mind is full of power. He can bring all minds under his influence; one is struck with awe and wonder at the marvels and mysterious powers of the mind of a man.

Man has lost most of his instinct, though it still plays a great role in our daily life. Even animals, such as dogs and cats, have lost much of their instinct because of their association with man, and subsequently, they suffer like man.

Even in sleep, the mind works without any rest and solves problems, arranges, classifies, compares, sorts all facts, and works out proper, satisfactory solutions. The mind is not limited by velocity; it can reach a distant star in a moment, for time and space are creations of the mind.

Good and evil are points of view; there is only power, energy, action, and will. Everything comes from the mind! We need to put religion back into the hands of the individual, because when they think they know the answers, people are difficult to guide; when they know they don't know, people can find their own way. The mind is an asymptotic expansion; by the year 2020 almost all overt tyranny will have been eliminated, because the mind and the universe will be tired of suffering under dogmatic belief systems.

King's Plea

Do not hold me accountable for my ancestors' merits
Nor their sins
Nor their thinking
Nor their spirits
Nor their ignorance.
I am not protected by their shrines
Nor protected by their love;
I am protected by the love of the eternal father-mother

That's the cry of your false
god dying
In Moses's days, devils were
your neighbors.
In Jesus's days, devils were in
the families.
In these days, devils are inside
of us.

Street Wars

Beware of a scoundrel,
for he devises evil, lest he give you a lasting blemish.

The People around the Corner

No good will come to the man who persists in evil
or to him who does not give alms.

They Talk Too Much

Better is a man who works and has an abundance of everything
than one who goes about boasting but lacks bread.

Greater Is the Simple Man

Many kings have had to sit on the ground,
but there are men never thought of that have worn a crown.

Be Positive

If you do kindness, know to whom you do it,
and you will be thanked for your good deeds.

Twenty-Five to Life with Pride

Whoever touches it will be defiled,
and whoever associates with a proud man will become like him.

Associating with the Wrong Things

What peace is there between a hyena and a dog?
And what peace is there between a rich man and a poor man?

Get out of Confusion

The man who fears those divine laws will do this,
and he who holds to the law will obtain wisdom.

Eighty-Five Percent of the World Lives in Poverty

The creator made man out of ghetto dust
And turned him back to it again.

The Wiles of the Media

The sinner is overtaken through his lips
The reviler and the arrogant are tripped by them

Running the Streets All Your Life

You have gathered nothing in your youth.
How then can you find anything in your old age?

The Blind, Deaf, and Dumb

I will again pour out teachings, like prophecies,
And leave it once again for all generations.

The Crumbs of Marriage

I would rather dwell with a lion and a dragon than dwell with
An evil wife or an evil husband

Savages and Drugs

Jealousy and anger shorten life
And anxiety brings on old age to soon

Look around You

Death is better than a miserable life
And eternal rest is better than chronic sickness

Simple Living

A man of cheerful and good heart will give heed to the food he eats.

Oppressors

woe to you, who love the deeds of unrighteousness

woe to you, who rejoice in the tribulation of the righteous

woe to you, who write down lying and godless words

woe to you, ye dark hearts, who work wickedness and eat blood

woe to you, ye fools, for through your folly ye shall perish

woe to you, who oppress the poor, your day of calamity is coming

woe to you, who rob and rape, for your seed shall have no rest

woe to those who build their houses with sin

woe to you, ye rich, for ye have trusted in your riches

woe to you, who requite your neighbor with evil

woe to you, lying witnesses

woe to you, who drink water from every fountain

woe to you, who devour the finest of foods

woe to man-made religions; your gods are false

The Change in Women

Women can discover God in their hearts, but they will have to search for the supreme mother in the hearts of other women.

Truth Overlooks Racism and Pride

Truth is timeless,
forever exempt from all transient vicissitudes.
Truth is never dead, it is formal,
always vibrant and alive.

Color and Pride

Too much racial pride destroys social development.

They Are Here

There are so many beings that hover around our galaxy.
There are about six hundred different beings that are living within the human solar system.
Out of six hundred, two hundred of them have visited the planet earth; not all of them are "good."

Worldly Knowledge Is Foolish

Always absorbed in self-knowledge, engaged in the study of philosophy and spirituality;
all this is declared as knowledge, and the rest is ignorance.

Too Much TV Warps the Mind

Whenever and wherever the mind becomes unsteady and unstable, then and there it must
be brought back under the control of the self.

The Wise Man and the Foolish Man

He who has controlled his self by his self, certainly his self is his best friend;
but for him who has not conquered his self, his self is his enemy.

Come as you Are people

It does not matter what religion you are; can you conquer Self?

Three Saviors (Opportunity, Blessings, Miracles)

The poor man looks for an opportunity
Greed wants a miracle
And the spiritual man awaits his blessings

Awe

Jesus sat in the yoga position, praying for the niyama spirit to help him understand his own dukkha.

Niyama—Purifying oneself through discipline
Dukkha—The belief that everything eventually leads to suffering

In the Pits of Babylon

Today I gave Yahweh seven hundred prayers of strength; across the baptismal times are more things searching for love and hope.

The King's Burial

Give me the heaviest of all strong wines for my burdens, lay me with
burdens, shed a tear on my tomb
Lead me to my eternal king, which is the one spirit
Write my sins with the unicorn pen
Love is here, but she is quiet

Ghetto Scrolls

After all, we really have no need for human Bibles, unless, sources of divine wisdom have been exhausted and proven insufficient to solve a problem that relates to the "reality."

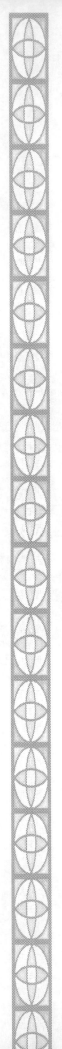

The Problems with the Old Church of Yesterday

Worshipping Jesus and the Virgin Mary has caused humanity to sink even deeper into the consciousness of separation and blindness, thus complicating the problems on earth instead of helping.
This has created more chaos to a downward movement.

In the Near Future

There are no race problems
Literally, all nations and races are of one blood
The brotherhood of man flourishes, and the nations are learning to live on earth in peace
and tranquility
Such a world stands on the eve of a great and culminating intellectual development

Individual Self-Control

For this shall be the new and living way; the joy of living takes on a new color, and the reaction of life are exalted to heavenly heights of tone and timbre.

The New System

For this shall be the era characterized by the worldwide pursuit of moral culture and spiritual truth. New systems of education and government grow up to supplant the crude and racist regimes of former times.

My Nation Has the Right Attitude

Pay attention to knowledge and seek for truths. Understand other races of people; love your goals and no one will harm you, nor will anyone try to rob you.

Dark Side of the Feminine

Her only sin was she loved darkness and all the meanings of darkness
To win love, she flirted with death
She could not bear to think of growing old and shriveled and worn out and
dying at last as hags die

Dark Alley

What do I see?
I see false priests and preachers forcing their doctrine of an outworn god
upon the people with fear and guilt.

America

It was a black reality, an empire of confusion, steeped in duality.
Soon it will be long forgotten. It was finally overthrown by men and women of poverty.
The priests, preachers, thugs, gangsters, prostitutes, terrorist, and psychological killers
practiced foul necromancy in their own ways, strange and backward ways of the most evil kind; grisly governments corrupt the people with a theocracy controlled by political wizards.

I Ask Jesus

"What is the Christ?"
Jesus said the Christ is the highest energy.
It is neither male nor female; any creature of thought can attain the Christ.

Rebel Love Song

There is no love, only rebel love

They abuse their love
They despise their love
They fear their love

Why won't you try this rebel love
      The only love
That will bring things rightfully back

      They destroy their love
      They hate their love
      They rearrange their love

Why won't you try this rebel love
      The only love
That will bring things rightfully back

Poor and Rich People Talking

All wisdom comes from the universe and it is with "it" forever.

Poverty Uprising

Righteous anger can be justified
For a people's anger tips the scale to its ruin

The Second America

I live in a country where there are so many churches and so many penitentiaries
and where the good man gets assassinated by registered assassins

Friends and Foes

Be not a hypocrite in man's sight
And keep watch over your lips

Hustling for the Right Thing

If you desire wisdom, keep the laws of the universe,
and it will supply you.

Another Genocide, for Another Race

HIV, crime, illiteracy, infant mortality, false religions, pop cultures, false history, and gangs

The Religion of Self-Knowledge

I will feel for my people
As I feel for myself
I will work out my own salvation by educating my brother man

Pan-Negroism

Teach me to drink the everlasting nectar of peace found in the foundations of Negroism.

What Affects One Man Will Affect All

Ignorance is at the root of our suffering
Ignorance arises in such forms as fear of death, hatred, and war
There is no such thing as independence; all living creatures are united in a symbiotic circle

The New African Americans (2020, the Year of the "Force of Love and Unity")

Thou despised me when I was weak.
Now that I am strong, ye comes? Verily, verily, neither my milk nor my harvest shall be for thee, but shall be for those who supported me in my tender age.

The Minds of Many People

The foul despise the things in life and seeketh heaven after death.

The Ghettos of India

African Americans also must know that their liberation struggle cannot be complete as long as their own blood-brothers and sisters living in far-off India are suffering.

Street Worship

Be aware of what you imagine, for eventually you will get it.

Walking in the Concrete Wilderness

You see, crime increases when crooks are in power, but law-abiding citizens will see them fall.

The Four Gospels: Jesus, Malcolm X, Buddha, and Marcus Garvey

No greater love than a man that will
lay down his life for his revolution.

Pure Mind

My mind is free of limitations
My mind is light and dark
Pure mind, what is it?

God Is "Force"

It surrounds us and penetrates us
It binds the galaxies together
It is what it is

A Warrior's Journey

The real walk in life
consists not in seeking new territory but in seeking with new eyes.

The Years AD 2012–4179

The galactic Diaspora is at hand
The human race has changed
God has revealed itself in a higher complexity
The higher good or the super good is beyond the religion of Jesus

Walking on the Throne Path

I will cultivate the calmness of one, knowing that the one spirit is ever with me; I am a living force.

Weeping Clouds

Time has been rearranged
Even fools shed tears
Death runs and hides
All diagrams of life have lost their masters—the coming of Mahdi

Jesus Christ, the Last Pantheon God

There's no hope here or here after in the ways of my people
You'd better watch your own back in heaven
In this world men and women suffer vainly, finding pleasure in the doctrines
of god and war

The Gods of the Bible, Koran, and Vedic

He dwells on a great mountain
What use is it to call on him
Little he cares if men or women die
Better to be quiet than to call their names
They will send you doom, not goodness
They are grim and loveless

The Skulls of Life

All the false gods roar and rage and dream
from all the brainwashing under the fear of human will
The gods want to help, they are not allowed to help

The Tears of King Solomon

Who can comfort my pain and my visions
Who can comfort my wisdom and my concubines
Who can spread their love over me like a bedcover
How can I please a thousand virgins

I live in misery because I did not search my true feelings

Mt. of Transfiguration

God is not …

Zen
Judaism
Christianity
Hinduism
Buddhism
Jainism
Sikhism
Shintoism
Taoism
Baha'I
Rastafarian
Islamic
Yoruba
Hebrew
Sadhu
Wicca

The Collapse of America

This indicates what may be expected when state undergoes too rapid extension
associated with internal degeneration

Listen, Children

The majority is not always right
Uneducated and indolent majorities have weak insight

What Is the Matter

No society has progressed very far when it permits idleness or tolerates poverty.

In the Valley of the Ghetto like Hebrews

In every age there will always be a rebel.
Men forget what is theirs and what is not,
allowing a rebel to come and take what was once his
rightfully back.

There Is an Old Mystic Flowing in the Christian Church

Some say, it's the sandals of Yeshua (Jesus)
Others say, the father-mother is about to freeze time
Children say, who are the real Christians?
The elders say, they have forgotten about the indigo language
The priests say, hell has lost his keys
The Nazirites say, the wood is wet and the fire is out
The scholars say, they have replaced the tetragrammatons with lies
Some say, the poor righteous is about to eat

The Expansion

Man has left the earth in the rockets of Babel. Alien races, seven more of Babylon's Equal star wars. Preaching the gospel to other worlds and galaxies will manifest Jesus Christ's kingdom.

Sayings from the Ancient Ghetto Streets

Do unto another what you would have him do unto you, and do not do unto another what you would not have him do unto you. Thou needest this law alone. It is the foundation of all the rest.
—Confucianism

Do nothing unto others which would cause you pain done unto you.
—Hinduism

Hurt not others in ways that you yourself would find hurtful.
—Buddhism

We would conduct ourselves toward others as we would have them act toward us.
—Greek

Do not do to others what you would not like others to do to you.
—Judaism

Whatever you wish that men would do to you, do so to them, for this is the law and the prophets.
—Christians

If it harms none, do what you want; how you treat me is how I treat you.
—The ghetto hoods and slums

Sci-Fi the Christ

Five hundred thousand sons of God (universe)
Which one is first
Who shall be the last
All of them are not human
They are the sources of light in all luminous objects
Galaxies beyond galaxies, dimensions beyond dimensions
Jesus is in the middle; who is the first?

The Usurper

Better to be slain by good than to be slain by evil
The sword of goodness liberates
The sword of evil does not liberate

Resurrection Is Rebirth

When one dies in the mode of ignorance, he takes birth in the animal
kingdom
There is no guarantee that the human being will again attain human status

The Real Afterlife

Those who are good gradually go upward to higher planets.
Those who are devotees live on earthly planets, and those who are ignorant
go down
to hellish planets, planets that are dead, like Mars and Mercury.

The Man of Simplicity Is So Real

Let pastors and preachers and philosophers argue over questions concerning life and reality
I already know this; if life is false, I am false
True this; this false living is real to me. I walk, I burn with love, I'm sexual, I kill, I live, I cry, and I am content.

All Things Begin in the Streets and Die in the Streets

So many Babylon cops
Time is twisted in the god of roots rock
So many street adventures have not been told
Alien technology has been sold
Priest and preachers are old-school wizards that are caught inside the
witches' bowl
The new age is already old
A rude black bent throne makes me bold
Gang banging is older than sin
Don't you see, I plea,
All religions are false in the third degree

Hither came the "Mighty Negro"
I'm high
Eyes are slit like an alien pharaoh
Skulls and crossbones have now found their true home
Children of poverty are still prone
I'm strong
America is the lost system of Rome
Mercenaries and warlords are camped out, waiting for the World War III
Dome
The old pagan way is gone
Planet X is the new Malcolm X
The right way is always long

Over-Man

Man is something that shall be overcome
What have I done to overcome this man of me
Everything in this universe has created something beyond itself
And man has not
I do not want to become a king
I want to become more than a man, I want to be the over-man

O God, Reduce My Worldly Drug Habits

I want to drug myself with the right kind of drugs
The only drugs are spiritual drugs that will help me come closer to the one spirit of truth

Community Problems

Teach me to feel that it is my smile manifesting in the dawn of darkness, on the edge of sweetness, and on the faces of the brokenhearted.

Too Much Marijuana and Alcohol

Forgive me, one spirit, for I have blocked the reception communion by putting too many chemical forces in my body.

I Have a (Disease) Dis-Ease

Today I will meditate on the one spirit, no matter how tired I am
I will not allow myself to feel dis-ease by the distracting noise that is around me

New Ideas in God Are Always Genuine

When love is taught with new ideas, life then becomes a breath of fresh air

I do not believe in God (gawd); I believe in the "I am"
I am god through the evolution of light
I am the way, the star, and the reincarnated
I am the offspring of time and rebirth
I am a citizen of Zion
I am the night-light of all electrons and protons
I am the thoughts of all antediluvian creatures
I am the strong arm of self
I am the morning dew for all races of children
I am the alien of many galaxies
I am the sub-absolute, pre-infinite, and the non-absolute
I am the religion of one
I am the thought adjusters of all times
I have no faith, I just believe
I do not believe in God (gawd) I believe in the I am

All Things Will Submit

When a man or woman overcomes thuggery,
They begin to accept realization in this vast universe.

Children Born in Prostitution

Though you may seem like an outcast and forgotten, society looks at you as being worse than the rotten; remember, God has a plan for your begotten seed, just look inside of yourself and see.

A Message to the Youth

In all that you do, eventually, it will catch up to you.

The Kingdom of Heaven

The kingdom of heaven will only come through strife, struggles, fights, wars, feuds, and suffering.

My Life Is Stronger Than Yours

Better off is a poor man who is well and strong in constitution than a rich man who is severely afflicted in body.

Every Day Is a Good Day

Why is any day better than another, when all the daylight in the year is from the sun?

All Things You Do in Life Acquire Work

When one builds and another tears down, what do they gain but toil?

The Good Treasure

He who acquires a wife gets his best possession, a helper fit for him and a pillar of support.

American Gangs

A funeral banquet has occurred
Early Christians destroyed the old burial customs
Some want to be cremated
While others argue that mummification
Is more suitable.

The Third Coming of Jesus
or
The Second Coming of the Church

Been living in ignorance for over eight hundred years
If love is true, why is there so much weeping dew?
If things were spoken well, why couldn't the children tell?
If the second coming is alive, why do we hope and cry?
If true worship was around, why do we persecute the unfounded?
This ungodly generation is looking up to God for selfish gain
and not helping to spread the love rain.
Some are looking for the second coming;
others are looking for the true church.

My Shabbat (Sabbath)

I am the heaven of this day

I am the tenth Christ on this day

I am the many messiahs on this day

Wisdom is I, and I am wisdom on this day

I am everything that Jesus was and is on this day

Sons of the Midnight Heavens

My breath
(oxygen)
is always a smokey prayer of thanks
that inhales the heavens
and exhales the elixirs of greatness

But without the sacred herb
(oxygen)
how can any living creature
say there is no love
(God)

Angelic Chancellor Sits and Writes

One hundred constellations
orbit around the divine heavenly warriors

Faithful hours
are the days and the rulers over the underground eternities

Beyond heaven and the heavens
the universal father and the high fathers
rarely see the one father.
He has appointed every living thing to rule;
he just peeps around the corner
every now and then.

The Tenth Epoch

Now is the time to leave the earth for good
Rebellions against God are frauds
War rebels and bloody politicians
fight over the last supper pods
Memories are buried in the old earth cobs
The new earth is waiting
for the next seed
to love and not to rob.

Another Look around the Corner

The doors are opening
in so many forms of light
The higher light
sits in dark void
Not all lights carry salvation

Five Riddles for the Sons of Men

Things thou hast seen
Things which are
Things shall be hereafter
Things of the now
and
Things that cometh in mystery

O Black India

The fruits have unfolded in the holy electrons
The tree of continuity lives in your black branches
Those who know God step into the first class of spirituality
Those who do not know God
Adapt to the ways of ignorance (animals)

Myth Is Always around the Corner

Myth is always knocking
on the civilized man's door
Magic is spellbound
and is taught even to the poor
Inspiration is not enlightenment
anymore
The truth comes in,
and myth still sleeps on the floor

Sikh Christians

O Nam
How excellent is thy name in all earth
Who set thy glory above the galaxies
We give you thanks
For the upper and lower gurus
Blessed be the teachings of Yeshua
And the deliverance of Guru Nanak
Sing praise to the timeless one
Which dwelleth in Zion:
He has shared his doing amongst the people of the earth
And his holy ones have saved us
By their Kesh offerings.

New Earth I

Dead love
may be preserved in primitive foolishness.
New love calls for a higher truth
and a different dynamic.
And the bed of life is finally fit
for the children
to understand the ignorance
of the past.

Indiafari

Selassie I dwells in the roots of Punjab
The children of Judah eat with the children of deep oppression
Love is always
Black
And mysterious
The words of reincarnation
Change the atoms of joy to the atoms of absolute
In the colorful East, the Nazirite men and women
See the morning star rise in peace
They all rally for the new baptism
That is taken place
in the black grass valleys

Living in a Trinity of Demigods

Time was never with man
Every trinity is a god,
And every god that controls time
is somewhat corrupted
Things live and die on natural times,
Everything does not die
on God's time

They Say Only Love Will Stand in the End

She will stand in the end,
but she will get abused again.
She will crush the head of her enemies,
but she has to redeem herself again.
She will get crucified again,
but she has to replenish herself again.
She will stand in the end,
with pain
and with a new name.

Dead God Scroll

The cosmos of the perfect man
Dwell in the higher lights of the Christs.
Many masters have come and brought intense teachings,
but the perfect light
is one arm,
one strength,
with Yah (God).

What Is Man, That Thou Art Mindful of Him

Man has evolved
from five hundred different types of human beings
that are and were living
in the galaxies.
Things in the unknown
are similar to man
and the son of one spirit
that thou has visited him in different eras.

In the Year of Roots Men

Every man has his own Garden of Eden
Every man's soul is a crystal crying tree
24, thee I plea
Elohim always sees
600 suns bow to their knees
Roots men in heaven sip black wisdom tea
The father of creation started dancing like a bee
75,000 heavens wanted to see

Mimicking the Sounds of Surroundings

The level of wind,
I can move swiftly without even thinking.
The different levels in a bird's chirps
are the movements of my body parts in action during war.
The level of quietness is a holy ritual.
The sound of a grasshopper
is the level of speaking through music.
The sound of rushing water
is the level of livity and a spiritual taste.
A flock of ravens
is the level of present
and the coming of your master.
The bee is motion and awareness.
The level of thunder is a death blow.
Listening to the levels and the sounds of wisdom, inside of wisdom
is a deadline.
The different levels of mimicking are the secrets
of the way things are.

Unseen Sins

Every day my right eye is in a meditating position,
Like Guru Nanak.
When will I wake up from this meditating crucifixion;
When will sin repent?
And who is going to relate to hate?

Keys

My soul is resting in the hundredth peace
Baptized in the river of decease
Now things begin to sleep
Your mind is a key to open the next peace

Under the Dead Space

Twenty thrones sit in the elliptical belt.
Nobody knows the soul of the extrasolar planets;;
beyond dark galaxies is more life.
Tidal waves in space roll to angelic music.
The path of the lonely comet,
nobody wants to take.
Auroras will shower hells instead of telling sweet tales.

All in Vain

Centuries-old cults
tried to find the unattainable secret
to life and wisdom,
but it only made Yahweh
put shackles on the corner stones
of pride and foolishness.

Here I Am, I Am Here

I will teach you peaceful things; here I am
If you stumble too hard, I am here
The spirits say, you can run but you can't hide—here I am Beautiful country
is all around us; I am here
Heaven is surrounded by all creatures; here I am
The ages of the world, I am here
The last words of Yeshua, here I am
The phases of the moon, I am here
I kneel only to the lion of Judah, here I am
You want to know the acts of a king—I am here
The blessing of the wise here I am Songs to disperse demons, I am here
Christians and Sikhs unite; here I am
Life is a mind warp; I am here Unification is a lost law; I am here
Who is your teacher? here I am
Does your maker love? I am here
Africa will unite, here I am
Remember me, I am here
Greed conquers all fear; there it goes
All things that are buried in time and in eras shall be raised;
there they are

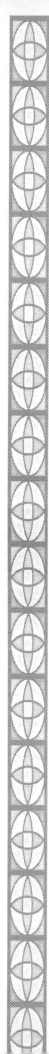

Nomad Christians

Wonder of miracles and walkers of cold nights;
in their hearts is the second coming,
but in their minds is more money.
Sleepers
beside the dead and the living,
adapters
of new ways and changes,
seeking to find lost souls
and seeking to please their father
and seeking to sit with all breadths of creations.

On the Other Side of Eternity

I'm too old to be a prophet
Too loving to be a child
Too glittering to be a star
Too much light to be a disciple
Too strong to be a king
Too many revelations to be a god
But I am just right to be father of

Matthew, Mark, Luke, John, and Paramahansa Yogananda

Five flowers try to grow.
Vampire weeds try to choke their growth.
The bonfires are still burning spiritually;
Roots and wisdom is their seat of content
Poverty is a virtue, but it can still hurt you.
Followers of the majority will never see the truth;
The five are back-to-back, side by side with the red lions, love Zion.

Herbal Christian Man

Burn the incense of livity
Show me the herbs of life
Give me the plants of the divine
Grow the trees of honey wisdom
Cure me with the leaves of healing
Bless me with the flowers of potion
Smoke the grass of medicine
Expand me to the roots of beauty
Spread the seed of righteousness over hard ground
Till the fields, sow time with the love of yeshua
And eat the bark of spiritual renewal.

The Philosophy of Time Is Carried on a Palanquin

Ancient tribes and scrolls are lost in the oceans;
the whole world was all green at one point.
Cuneiform tablets of different tribes after and before
the flood
are buried in screams.
Scrolls of biblical lost animals;
good and evil are lost to ancient Bibles
and time travelers are lost in the canyons and in valleys of oceans and seas.
Geometry of math and unknown medicines vanish as well.
Technology was already there;
everything goes up and down in a fixed-point arrangement.
Perhaps there may have been scrolls on flying machines that man recorded,
races beyond space,
praising our god,
but carrying a different Bible with strange elilim sins?
Paranormal things wander around;
all things in the earth man will never know.
Know yourself so you can be known,
because how, what, when, and where will control you forever.

The Last Image of God (Yah)

Everything has its own image
as well as its own wisdom.
Colors divide time through the math of love,
and images are
the beginning of the first and last steps with Yah.

Avidya
(Spiritual ignorance, a cause of much suffering)

I dieth not to myself
Who do I trust—not myself
Who created me—not myself
Who is my security—not myself
I am the truth; I dieth not to myself
Who is my future—not myself
I dieth not to my spirit or to my soul

Who's That in the Sky?

Rastafarians say It's Selassie I

Muslims say It's the Messenger

Egyptians say It's the Star of Thoth

Greeks say It's the fall of Hercules

Sikhs say It's the spirit of Guru Nanak

Hindus say Moksha has reached It's highest liberations

The children say It's Yeshua (Jesus)

Three Christs

I will love them according to the integrity of my heart

I will bathe the children according to the integrity of my heart

I will show them perpetual living according to the integrity of my heart

The Six Visions

Though I have the gift of making the sea kiss my lips
and have not loved,
I am nothing

Though I have the gift of opening times
and have not loved,
I am nothing

Though I have the gift of love
and have not loved,
I am nothing

Though I have the gift of turning a sour day into a blessed day
and have not loved,
I am nothing

Though I have the gift of making the moons pregnant
and have not loved,
I am nothing

Though I have the gift of wings
and don't know how to fly,
I am nothing

Unlearned

Love is light
It takes flight Blinds you slightly
Not so quietly
Too much of this will burn you precisely

Peaceful Revolution

In times of greed,
Let's plant a seed
For the children.
When we are confused,
Let's pick up reality
And deal with the bruise.
Oral teachings are my revolution,
Not beautiful pollution.

The Cycles of Creations
(before the existing of man)

Ye should know, children,
that the color of love is in everything
that is Christ-like.

True enlightenment is helping the poor,
and the true church is not a religion.

The Evolution of Salvation

Salvation shall be preached to all tongues of people
by different men from different religions,
holding the four flowers in their hands:
truth, wisdom, justice, and righteousness.

On the day of reckoning,
all religions will be judged.

What is the Fourth Density?

A "density" is best described as an ontological plane of existence, of which there are seven. The meaning of each of these planes/densities depends upon the system of philosophy that references them, and each has various attributes. Most are associated with the colors of the rainbow, and have these basic meanings:

Density	Color	Theosophic Plane	
7	Violet	Divine, masters	Unity
6	Indigo	Monadic, archangels	Wisdom
5	Blue	Nirvanic/Atmicangels and demons,	Honor
4	Green	Buddhic, ethical/spiritual man	Love
3	Yellow	Mental,animal and human, biological kingdom	Spirit
2	Orange	Astral,plant, lower biological kingdom	Mind
1	Red	Physical, mineral, inanimate kingdom	Body

In this material, we use the "density" structure described by those of Ra in the *Law of One* books and material, which is basically a quantum level of complexity. The higher the density, the higher the complexity of the structures it contains.

The earth currently exists in the first, second and third densities; the mineral kingdom comprising the first; plants and lower animals, the second; higher animals and mankind, the third. The earth is currently in transition to the fourth density, which is typically referred to as a new paradigm of understanding.